Printed in China
02 03 04 05 06 07 08 LEO 8 7 6 5 4 3 2

Lyrics for *The American Girls Anthem* by Gretchen Cryer
Music for *The American Girls Anthem* by Nancy Ford
Quotes from the American Girls stories by Valerie Tripp,
Janet Shaw, Connie Porter, and Susan Adler
Illustrations by Dan Andreasen, Nick Backes, Bill Farnsworth,
Renée Graef, Walter Rane, Dahl Taylor, and Jean-Paul Tibbles

Visit our Web site at **americangirl.com**

Lindsay — I know you will be the best that you can be.
Love, Nana

the *Best* that I CAN BE

A MESSAGE *to* PARENTS

FOR OVER A DECADE, The American Girls Collection has encouraged girls to be their very best. Through stories about Kaya, Felicity, Josefina, Kirsten, Addy, Samantha, Kit, and Molly, girls realize that they're part of a long, proud line of daughters, mothers, and grandmothers who have profoundly affected their country and their world. *The Best That I Can Be* is the essence of all the goodness, hope, and heart in the American Girls stories. Full of wisdom and kindness, the quotes in this little book both inspire and guide girls, showing them that they, too, can meet today's challenges with strength and courage.

the *Best* that I CAN BE

the AMERICAN GIRLS ANTHEM

Look to the past,
Learn for the future.
Look to the past,
Learn for the future.
I can be brave,
I can be true,
I will do the best
that I can do.
And I can dream,
I can dare,
I can keep on trying
if I really care.
If I reach out,
I can belong.
I can be a friend,
Lend a helping
hand so strong.
I'll hang on to my dreams,
Flying high and free,
And I will be the best
that I can be.

I can be brave,
I can be strong
When I'm alone or
something's going wrong.

I'll do what's right,
I can be true,
I will keep on going,
and I'll carry through.

I'll use my head,
I can be fair,
I can be a friend,
I can really show I care.
I'll sing with my
own voice,
The voice inside of me,
And I will be the best
that I can be.

I won't let one mistake
discourage me.
I can be brave,
I can be strong,
I can be kind,
Make up my mind.
I can reach out,
I can belong,
Sing my own song.

I can be true,
And follow through.
I can be fair,
I can dream,
I can dare,
I can share,
I can be free,
I can be me.

I can be brave,
I can be true,
I will do the best
that I can do.
And I can dream,
I can dare,
I can keep on trying
if I really care.
If I reach out,
I can belong,
I can be a friend,
Lend a helping hand
so strong.
I'll hang on to my dreams,
Flying high and free.
Yes, I will be the best
that I can be.

I can be
brave,
I can be true,

Penny can't jump that fence, *Felicity thought.* ***It's too high.*** *But with one graceful leap, Penny jumped and sailed over the highest rail.*
"Go on," whispered Felicity. "Go on, Penny. You are free."

—Meet Felicity

I will do the best
that I can do.

The dog sighed, and looked at Kit with the saddest eyes she'd ever seen. "Stirling, this dog's been abandoned," she said. "We've got to bring her home and feed her."

—HAPPY BIRTHDAY, KIT!

And I can dream,
I can dare,

"You'll need much strength in the days ahead if you're to work as your namesake did to feed the people. Now it's time for you to wear this." Kautsa placed the hat firmly on Kaya's head.

"I'm ready, Kautsa," Kaya said.

—Changes for Kaya

I can keep on trying
if I really care.

Keep going, Kirsten told herself. She began to count the way Miss Winston drilled numbers in school. **One, two, three, four**—that was four steps closer to home.

—KIRSTEN'S SURPRISE

If I reach out,
I can belong.

"I think Sam's sense of value is just fine, Mother," interrupted Uncle Gard quietly. "She gave the doll to Nellie."

Grandmary nodded slowly. "Yes, I think Samantha's sense of value is just fine indeed."

—MEET SAMANTHA

I can be a friend,
Lend a helping
hand so strong.

Kaya held tightly to Steps High's mane. She'd have to catch Speaking Rain as soon as she came within reach, or else Speaking Rain would be swept under the horse's sharp hooves. Kaya reached and grasped, caught her arm—she had her!

—Meet Kaya

I'll hang on
to my dreams,
Flying high
and free,

*Molly beamed. She couldn't wait until the next night. Miss LaVonda would see: Molly would dance even **better** when Dad was in the audience!*

—CHANGES FOR MOLLY

And I will be the
best that I can be.

"Here," said Josefina.
At first, the goat seemed
too weak even to open
her mouth. But then
she sucked the milk
off Josefina's fingers.
"That's it," said Josefina.
"That's the way."

—HAPPY BIRTHDAY, JOSEFINA!

I can be brave,
I can be strong

Addy turned just in time to see her mother disappear beneath the churning water. Addy wanted to scream, but she kept it inside. Instead, she drew in air, filling her lungs, and dove under the water.

—MEET ADDY

When I'm alone
or something's
going wrong.

*Kit didn't budge.
She'd promised Mother
that she would help.
It would take more than
Uncle Hendrick's bluster
and Inky's snarls
to discourage her.*

—Kit's Surprise

I'll do
what's right,
I can be true,

"If our factories can hurt children, then we have not made good progress in America," Samantha continued. "And I want to believe Americans want to be good. I believe we want to be kind. And if we are kind, I believe we will take care of the children."

—Samantha Learns a Lesson

I will keep on going,
and I'll carry through.

Josefina put her hand on Papá's arm, and he patted it while he stared into the fire. So many sheep killed! The rancho could not survive without sheep. What would Papá do?

—JOSEFINA LEARNS A LESSON

I'll use my head,
I can be fair,

Kaya had an idea. Perhaps she and Two Hawks could escape together. Two would have a better chance to make it over the mountains than one traveling alone.

—KAYA'S ESCAPE!

I can be a friend,
I can really
show I care.

Molly thought making the skirts had been lots of fun. Susan showed them how to make crepe paper flowers that were big and colorful. Mrs. McIntire even squirted some of her perfume on the girls!

—MEET MOLLY

I'll sing with
my own voice,
The voice
inside of me,

Addy started to speak, and the words came easily. Her voice was loud and clear as she read the proclamation, with its words that had changed the lives of everyone she loved.

—CHANGES FOR ADDY

And I will be the
best that I can be.

Kaya hugged the beautiful saddle of painted wood and hide. But her mind couldn't take in the second gift that Swan Circling had given. Her name! That was the greatest gift anyone could give.

—KAYA'S HERO

I won't let one mistake
discourage me.

Felicity took a small bite of the hard biscuit. As soon as she chewed, she knew it was a mistake. Her loose tooth fell out and landed—Plop! Clink!—in her cup of tea.

—FELICITY LEARNS A LESSON

I can be brave,
I can be strong,

I'll have to swim underwater. Molly shuddered.
I can't make myself do it, she thought. But Linda was
coming closer and closer and closer . . . Quickly, Molly
took a deep breath and slid down under the surface.

—MOLLY SAVES THE DAY

I can be kind,
Make up my mind.

The kitten's heart beat like the flutter of a butterfly wing. Kirsten moved the kitten closer to Missy. "Oh, yes, that kitten will make it," Kirsten whispered. "You'll see."

—HAPPY BIRTHDAY, KIRSTEN!

I can reach out,
I can belong,
Sing my own song.

Josefina listened very hard. It seemed to her that the music helped her remember the sound of Mamá's voice, and so she was glad to hear it.

—JOSEFINA'S SURPRISE

I can be true,
And follow
through.

"I'll bring you more food," Kaya whispered. "You asked me for help, and I'll give it. I promise."

—KAYA AND LONE DOG

I can be fair,
I can dream,

"I gave Lydia to my friend Nellie. She had never owned a doll in her life. Not ever!" Samantha took one last look at the doll in the window, then shook her head. "I just don't think Grandmary would buy me another doll so soon."

—SAMANTHA'S SURPRISE

I can dare,
I can share,

Kit held on for dear life. Then, as suddenly as it had appeared, the train was gone, screaming off into the dark. **I've got to get home,** she told herself over and over again. **I've got to get help for Stirling and Will.**

—Kit Saves the Day

I can be free,
I can be me.

If I whistled loud enough,
Felicity thought, Nan and everyone in
Williamsburg would hear me. They'd see
me up here on the roof, as high as a flag!
She smiled. **Wouldn't that be fine?**

—Felicity Learns a Lesson

I can be brave,
I can be true,

It was probably like this the night my parents drowned, *Samantha said to herself.* **She shivered. We've got to get through this passage,** *Samantha thought.*

—SAMANTHA SAVES THE DAY

I will do the best
that I can do.

Dad was home from work! Kit snatched
up her newspaper, flew downstairs,
and burst out the door. "Extra! Extra!
Read all about it!" she shouted.

—MEET KIT

And I can dream,
I can dare,

It was as if Mamá herself were encouraging Josefina to learn to read and write. Francisca was wrong. Reading and writing wouldn't pull them away from Mamá, it would help them remember her.

—JOSEFINA LEARNS A LESSON

I can keep on trying
if I really care.

"Here, sit down,"
Samantha said. "We're
going to get you out of
second grade, Nellie.
Put Lydia on the
window seat and
let's get started."

—SAMANTHA LEARNS A LESSON

If I reach out,
I can belong,

Molly moved closer to Emily. She knew how it felt to be worried about someone far away and in danger. "My dad's there, too," she said. "I miss him so much my heart hurts."

—HAPPY BIRTHDAY, MOLLY!

I can be a friend,

*"**My** tepee." Singing Bird stood and stretched her arms wide to show Kirsten she spoke of a real tepee. Kirsten's heart sped up. Singing Bird wanted her to go to the Indian village!*

—KIRSTEN LEARNS A LESSON

Lend a helping
hand so strong.

"Oh, Harriet," Addy said with a sigh as she sank to her knees. She reached out her hand and gently touched Harriet's knee. "I'm so sorry," she said. "I truly am. I know you loved your uncle. I know you were proud of him."

—ADDY SAVES THE DAY

I'll hang on
to my dreams,

Felicity's eyes filled with happy tears.
She reached up and put her arms around
Penny's neck. "I knew we would find each
other again someday," Felicity whispered.

—FELICITY SAVES THE DAY

Flying high
and free.

Mrs. McIntire tried hard to keep her voice calm, but it was so full of happiness it sounded wobbly. She read, "I'm coming home…" and everyone exploded. "HURRAY! YIPPEEE! DAD! DAD! DAD!"

—CHANGES FOR MOLLY

Yes, I will be
the best
that I can be.

Kit held the newspaper
in her two hands.
Thousands of people
would read words that
she had written. Kit
shivered with delight.
She could hardly
believe it was true.

—CHANGES FOR KIT

ARE THERE TIMES when you've felt as brave as Felicity when she sets Penny free? Or as generous as Samantha when she gives her precious doll to Nellie? On the next pages, American girls like you share stories that will inspire you to stand proud, reach high, and be your very best!

that I CAN BE

When someone asks me to do my best, I feel that they trust me or depend on me, and I like that. When I was at the state swim meet, my team was counting on me to win a race, and I won. I think it was the faith they put in me.

HANNAH, LOUISIANA

Best

Whenever I sit down to do a school assignment that I really want to do well on, I say to myself, "Okay, do your best here." I get comfortable, sharpen my pencil, and start to work really slowly without rushing. At the end, I read it through for mistakes. It really works!

EMILY, ENGLAND

You should try to be your best all the time! The best of YOU is the best!

LEIGHELA, FLORIDA

I think I am my very best when I am singing or playing the piano. When my aunt died, my grandparents were so sad. I took my piano books to their house and played some of my slow, soothing pieces. Both of my grandparents came and stood beside me while I was playing. They said that my music was one of the most soothing things they had had for a long time. I was so happy that I had cheered them up a little.

LESLIE, ARKANSAS

The best thing I have ever done was to write a hero paper about my mom for school. After I finished, she was really pleased and was very touched by it. So, tell your parents you appreciate them, because they appreciate what you say.

CAPHINA, ENGLAND

In my first competition for marching bands, I kept my flute so high up and pulled my toes up so high (which is what we are supposed to do). My teacher said, "You kept it up, you kept it up!" It really made me feel great inside!

SAMANTHA, NEW JERSEY

Being your best means standing
up for what you know is right,
even when it's not the popular thing
to do. Afterward, you'll feel great.

KATIE, VIRGINIA

While I'm running the track or climbing rope, I always say to myself, "I can do it!" over and over again. It helps me do my very best!

ROSE, MINNESOTA

When I play softball, being my best means that I am encouraging my teammates, never giving up, and preparing myself properly before the game. That way, I always feel like a winner!

PARISA, FLORIDA

I am the editor of my classroom newspaper. Possibly my favorite time of all time is when I stood at the front of the class after I'd handed out the first issue and everyone applauded me.

ANNIE, ILLINOIS

When someone asks me to be my best, I try my hardest. I know that being my best doesn't mean being better than someone else, but being the best version of me.

MORGAN, ILLINOIS

The time when I was my very best was when I got home from school one day, and, instead of complaining, I offered to do the lunch dishes. I got big smiles from my mom and dad, and that made me smile and feel even better.

KARA, CALIFORNIA

A time when I had to be the best I could be was after my mom had a baby. It made me feel wonderful that I could actually help! My parents were really proud of me.

PATRICIA, MICHIGAN

I felt I was doing my best when we were playing our last soccer game of the season against my friend's team. We hadn't won a single game. I was a forward and racing for the goal. I dodged the defender and shot. It was the first goal I had ever made in my four years of playing soccer! Later, my friend told me after that she had been silently cheering for me.

ALYSSA, UTAH

I think that being your best doesn't necessarily mean winning the competition or finishing your test faster than the rest of the class. Instead, focus on trying to beat YOUR records, and getting as many answers correct as possible. Be YOUR best, not your friends', or your classmates'.

AN AMERICAN GIRL

Doing your best does not always mean being the best at something.
I have pretty bad asthma. When I run, I can't breathe very well. I hated doing the run we do every week at school. I decided I was going to try to run one mile in the 12 minutes we run. I tried really hard, and I got one and a quarter miles! I was one of the slowest runners, but I still was so proud.

NATALIE, ILLINOIS

When someone asks me to be and do my best, I always sit up tall. Being my best is working hard in school and doing chores or getting along with siblings at home. And don't forget: Being your best does *not* mean to be perfect.

HOLLY, NORTH CAROLINA

To be your best means to put your whole heart, mind, and soul into what you are striving to achieve. Remember, "Do your best, and you have met with success!"

LETTI, WYOMING

RECORDING CREDITS

Producer . . . . .Arnold Roth

Lyrics . . . . .Gretchen Cryer

Music . . . . .Nancy Ford

Arranger and Orchestrator . . . . .Bruce Coughlin

Music Director/Conductor/Piano . . . . .Jamie Schmidt

Music Contractor . . . . .AWR Music LLC/Arnold Roth

Music Preparation . . . . .Kaye-Houston Music Inc.
Jet Music Preparation

Casting Director . . . . .Rick Boynton

Talent Coordinator . . . . .Shelley J. Crosby

Recording Studios . . . .Chicago Recording Co., Chicago, Illinois
Master Sound, Astoria, New York

Recording Engineers . . . . .Chris Sabold
Ben Rizzi

Assistant Recording Engineers . . . . .Dennis Tousana
David Merrill

Mastering . . . . .Konrad Strauss

Special thanks to Susan Zilber and Elizabeth Richter